The Spirituality of Parenting

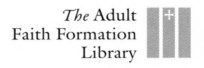

The Adult
Faith Formation
Library

The SPIRITUALITY of PARENTING

Connecting Heart and Soul

KATHY HENDRICKS

TWENTY
THIRD 23rd
PUBLICATIONS
www.23rdpublications.com

Twenty-Third Publications

1 Montauk Avenue, Suite 200, New London, CT 06320
(860) 437-3012 » (800) 321-0411 » www.23rdpublications.com

ISBN: 978-1-62785-127-5
Library of Congress Catalog Card Number: 2015952057
Printed in the U.S.A.

The Adult
Faith Formation
Library

F ormation in our faith tradition is an ongoing endeavor; allowing this learning to inform our minds,
to touch our hearts, and to find expression in the
way we live is an essential part of this process. *The
Adult Faith Formation Library Series* offers a valuable collection
of titles that are a reliable resource for formation, information,
and transformation in the Catholic tradition.

The Series is perfect for

- Adults in a faith community who would like to
  grow through spiritual reading and reflection

- Parish/pastoral ministers who seek support in
  their personal and professional development

- Pastoral teams or school faculties who desire
  to enrich or further explore their mission

- Individuals who want to deepen their
  own understanding of the faith

Each volume's user-friendly format provides

- An introduction to the topic

- Four chapters, each designed for reading in one sitting/ session

- Questions for personal reflection and journaling, or for conversation starters in a team or learning community

- A suggested reading list for further exploration

Boston College's STM Online: Crossroads (**www.bc.edu/ crossroads**) uses this series in its innovative course-style learning program. Crossroads gathers participants from the English-speaking world and creates learning communities that discuss the book together online. Pacing the conversation by using a chapter a week, a facilitator keeps the conversation going, encourages deeper discussion, and inquires how the reading inspires new or renewed spiritual practice. These popular courses are used as adult faith formation tools and as professional development experiences for ministers.

Whether used in formal educational settings or in less formal learning communities, *The Adult Faith Formation Library Series* offers faith formation in an accessible, flexible format for those who seek to live their faith in vibrant and informed ways in today's world.

CONTENTS

INTRODUCTION   I

CHAPTER ONE   7

The Vigilant Heart

CHAPTER TWO   25

The Joyful Heart

CHAPTER THREE   43

The Heavy Heart

CHAPTER FOUR   63

The Hopeful Heart

EPILOGUE   77

RESOURCES   81

Dedication

For Jenny, Eric, Anna,
and the baby we never knew.
Each of you expanded my heart in ways
I never thought possible.

INTRODUCTION

"BEING A PARENT MEANS WALKING AROUND WITH YOUR HEART OUTSIDE YOUR BODY FOR THE REST OF YOUR LIFE." This quote has made its way around parenting circles in various forms for years. It expresses the heartfelt experience of parenting, one entailing vulnerability and a letting go of outcomes and control. It's not a role for the faint of heart.

There are over one thousand references to the heart in the Bible, more than those referring to the body, the mind, or even the soul. The Hebrew word for heart, *lev*, denoted the seat of wisdom and understanding. It encompassed the vast range of human emotion, something we continue to associate in metaphoric fashion with the heart today. In addition to understanding the heart as the emotional center of an individual, *lev* included the collective mind, or mind-set, of the people. It was, in essence, the mental heart as well as one of flesh. The heart was the spiritual meeting place between God and God's people. In his book *The Awakened Heart*, Gerald May describes the heart as the place "where we are in most intimate contact with God's presence and with our essential union with others, where the deep, ongoing love affair be-

1

tween God and human beings actually takes place."

One of the most beautiful references to this connecting place is the passage from Ezekiel: "A new heart I will give you, and a new spirit I will put within you; and I will remove from your body the heart of stone and give you a heart of flesh" (Ezekiel 36:26). An enfleshed heart pulses, throbs, and beats in rhythm with God's own heart. I once heard this passage likened to a spiritual heart transplant. It entails conversion—a change of heart—something that is ongoing in the lives of those who seek to enter into God's heart. Jesus called for such conversion by inviting his followers to enter into love—love of God, love of others, love of self.

The heart *in love*—one immersed in love—is a heart that has gone outside of itself. The object of one's love becomes the focal point, and all sorts of energy are directed toward that relationship. While we usually associate falling in love with a romantic relationship, it can also be applied to the parent who falls in love with his or her child at the moment of meeting. Over the years, a range of emotions unfolds and draws the parent's heart outward in joyous, strange, frightening, wondrous, and mysterious ways.

Parenting and the States of the Heart

The term "spirituality" might seem a bit overwhelming when juxtaposed with the day-to-day reality of parenting, particularly when children are moving in and out of phases and stages that baffle the mind. Nonetheless, parenting as a spiritual endeavor resonates with a transformative movement of the heart. This makes the experience rich ground for spiritual growth and reflection. Parents lay a foundation for the faith of their children but are also formed and shaped by God in the process. This happens through the very ordinary tasks of raising children and guiding them toward adulthood. Each task is rooted in the sacred. Ezekiel's image of a heart plucked out of the body and then placed back makes an apt description of a parent's heart.

There is no shortage of books about how parents form, educate, and nurture their children, particularly in religious and spiritual values. I have added to the mix myself with books on faith formation and prayer in the home. There seem to be very few books, however, inviting parents to reflect on their role and to nourish their own spirituality in the midst of their busy and complicated lives. Such is the purpose of this book. Thus, it won't contain a lot of helpful hints about managing family life; rather, it will offer insights into how a parent can care for his or her own heart.

While children go through various stages and phases in the course of growing up, parents do too. These are not necessarily sequential, however, and they include, at the deepest spiritual level, an expansion of the heart. It might be more appropriate to describe the movement of a parent's heart as one of "states" versus stages. The next four chapters will examine four **states of the heart**: **vigilance, joy, heaviness**, and **hope**. In each one, the heart of parenting will be explored as we look at ways in which the heart expands, rejoices, breaks open, and sometimes shatters as children are anticipated, born or adopted, raised, and let go.

The challenge of parenting is as old as history, and so we find it embedded in the Scriptures. The "first parents," Adam and Eve, set the stage as their sons duke out their conflicts to a bloody and tragic end. Happily, the challenges most parents face will not be as extreme. Even so, they tax the heart. They are also offset by the blessings that come with parenting— the joy, pride, and moments of delight that arise in watching children grow into themselves. **Scriptural stories** lay a foundation for these blessings and challenges. Thus, each chapter of this book includes a connection with parents in the Bible, especially Mary, and how they embody the states of the heart.

The African proverb "It takes a village to raise a child" is another familiar adage. For many parents today, however, the "village" is shrinking. Households have become more mobile and, as a result, less connected with extended family and neighborhoods. Such mobility weakens the connection with institutions that support the family, such as churches and schools. This situation makes the value of **companionship** all the more vital. The need for support systems, particularly through the parish and school, is critical. Companioning is also an essential component of spiritual growth and development. As the states of the heart are examined in each chapter, I will offer ideas about particular companions who bolster the heart of the parent.

I don't know any parent who went through a training program prior to welcoming a child into their lives. Parenting is pretty much a learn-as-you-go endeavor. What often takes us by surprise is the way in which particular **gifts** of the heart arise as we meet the challenges and bask in the blessings of parenthood. Each of the four chapters will offer a look at some particularly important gifts that help a parent move more deeply into their roles and relationships. One gift common to all states of the heart is **prayer**, and so I will also offer ideas for various spiritual practices pertinent to parents.

My husband, Ron, is a trail runner. Every once in a while I see him standing still and holding a finger to the pulse at the side of his neck in order to check his heart rate. This is a marvelous metaphor for the spiritual life. By taking our spiritual pulse on a regular basis, we become more aware of ways to maintain a **healthy heart**. This is particularly important for parents who find themselves spent at the end of a day and too exhausted to tend to their own needs. Caring for others, particularly children, is a demanding task. I don't know how we go about it effectively if we aren't careful to mind the state of our own hearts. Ideas for doing so could fill another book. Instead of trying to cover the entire spectrum of self-care for parents, however, each chapter concludes with ideas for maintaining good spiritual health and how to tend each state of the heart.

While the primary reader of this book is the parent, it is also written for those who walk alongside parents as family members, friends, neighbors, ministers, and coworkers. **Questions** at the end of each chapter invite reflection and discussion to help both parents and those supporting them deepen their understanding of the spirituality of parenting.

ONE

The VIGILANT
HEART

"Quickening" is the moment during pregnancy when a woman first starts to feel or perceive the movements of her child. It's akin to the fluttering of butterfly wings—almost imperceptible but nevertheless real. I have given birth to three children, and with each one the quickening was a moment of heightened awareness. It made the expectation of a baby less ethereal. It helped me recognize that I wasn't going to *be* a mother; I already was one.

During my first pregnancy, my mother-in-law sent me the *Better Homes and Gardens Baby Book*. Over the next several months, I pored over each chapter, particularly the ones detailing the baby's growth and development. Each stage brought a new wave of anticipation and awe. The BH&G book predat-

7

ed *What to Expect When You're Expecting,* the ultimate how-to guide to pregnancy that sold millions of copies and inspired a movie of the same name. While the information in the BH&G book was less extensive, I was still mesmerized by its description of fetal development. Thus I tracked with wonder my child's growth from zygote to embryo to fetus and then the transition from womb to the world through childbirth. The latter was heightened by participation in Lamaze classes in which each phase of the birthing process was described in fascinating, and somewhat terrifying, detail. What neither book nor class could prepare me for, however, was the after-birth experience of being with my newborn baby. It's a breath-taking experience that leaves a parent changed in ways she or he could never have imagined.

Expectant parents—be it those awaiting the birth of a child or arrival through adoption or remarriage—learn to watch while they wait, attentive to the movement of the child into their lives. There are many such parents in the Bible. Abraham and Sarah give up on their dream of having a child until an unexpected guest tells them to wait just a little bit longer. Hannah, throughout years of infertility, prays fervently for a son and awaits an answer after promising that he will lead a life of consecrated service to God. Elizabeth and Zechariah are stunned by news of a child that will be given to them in their old age. And, of course, Mary receives the incredible news of her impending motherhood through the working of the Holy Spirit. Rather than knowing exactly what to expect, each figure remains open to the workings of God in their lives.

Mary's "yes" in the account of the Annunciation opens

the door to redemption. She cooperates with the divine plan, thus becoming a critical part of the incarnational event— God made flesh. Her openheartedness is all the more touching when one recalls that she was just a young girl—perhaps only thirteen—when she received the startling news from an angel. Nevertheless, her song of praise for a God who has asked more than she could imagine is a model of faith and trust. "My soul magnifies the Lord and my spirit rejoices in God my Savior..." (Luke 1:46–47). The exuberance in her prayer is an exquisite illustration of her abiding love for God and respect for God's inscrutable ways.

The Sanctity of Vigilance

I once read an article that described vigilance as the most defining characteristic of a saint. While the saints shine in particular ways through their piety, generosity, compassion, mercy, or commitment to justice, it's their willingness to wait upon God's time that draws them all together.

I know a lot of parents who qualify for sainthood by dint of this description alone. All parents know in some way, however, what it means to be vigilant. Consider the various types of vigils parents keep, from awaiting the initial arrival of a baby into the household to a teenager making it home safely from a first date. While the expectant parent is associated with pre-birth moments, other forms of expectation arise throughout a child's life. Parents understand the need to be vigilant—to expect and anticipate, to wait and endure, to remain attentive and alert to a child's feelings, moods, needs, wants, and growth. It's at one and the same time the most agonizing part of parenting and the most wondrous. Sometimes it feels as if you'll never again get a good night's sleep. At other times it makes you feel as if you have finally woken up to life. I wouldn't trade it for the world.

I gained another insight into vigilance while directing a women's retreat on openheartedness. The parish priest provided an entrée into the theme by showing a picture of himself as a toddler. He was just learning to walk and the photo showed his father holding his hands as he struggled to keep upright. The priest then asked the mothers to describe the experience of teaching their children to take their first steps. "There was a lot of bending over," one responded.

That "bending over" extends throughout a parent's life. Sometimes it reaches extremes, as in the case of "helicopter parenting"—the tendency to hover a tad too much and thus impede a child's movement into independence. When kept in balance, however, the protective love of a parent is vital to a child's well-being. One of the most beautiful passages in the Bible is the account of Jesus' baptism, when the sky above him opens and "the Spirit of God [descends] like a dove..." (Matthew 3:16). The image is akin to a mother dove hovering over her nest, beating her wings to keep her hatchlings safe. It's a touching illustration of the "bending over" that is intrinsic to parenting.

Different Kinds of Vigilance

My BH&G book also didn't prepare me for the unexpected turns along a parent's road. The day after she was born, the doctor told us our little Jenny had Down syndrome. A few weeks later she was diagnosed with an underdeveloped colon that required immediate surgery and left her with a colostomy. The latter condition threw Ron and me into a different kind of vigilance—that of sitting by an ailing child's bedside. It was a time of heart-stopping anxiety.

After her recovery, still another form of vigilance took hold. I set aside the BH&G book, with its neat and tidy stages of a child's first two years of development, and opened myself to discovery. Jenny was born in 1977. At the time terms like "special needs" and "mentally and physically challenged" were not yet part of everyday parlance. Down syndrome was a mysterious term as well and, since we didn't know what to expect, we watched and waited as Jenny grew in her own time and way. Down syndrome opened a door for us into the lives of parents who have a whole different understanding of "normal." Even though I didn't articulate it at the time, I was experiencing a "bent over" God who watched over us with tenderness and love. It was the infusion of the Divine into our everyday lives, something the fourteenth-century mystic Julian of Norwich described in one of her beautiful visions. "See that I am God. See that I am in all things…See that I have never stopped ordering my works, nor ever shall, eternally. See that I lead everything on to the conclusion I ordained for it, before time began, by the same power, wisdom and love with which I made it. How should anything be amiss?"

After Jenny recovered from her surgery, life took on a normalcy that would characterize any new parent's household. Aside from learning to change her colostomy bag, taking care of her was no different than what we did for her two siblings—Eric and Anna—who came along later. Routines were set in place and everyday tasks became mundane.

Everyday vigilance can trigger different reactions. For me, it was relief. I was happy to trade the vigilance of the hospital for that of the home. For other parents, however, it can be a time of strain and self-doubt. In an issue of the Christian spiritual journal *Weavings*, author Gayle Boss describes the experience of many stay-at-home parents in which each day seems to resemble the next. "It's not so much the relentless-ness of meals and all the mop-up that gets me muttering. It's the boredom. Another desert mile that looks just like the last desert mile" ("Leaning Forward," *Weavings*, XVIII, No. 2). Within a society that judges people by their economic worth, parenting can feel like an endless desert walk. Even so, there is inestimable value in the parent's role. The repetitive work of parenting, Boss notes, is also redemptive. God had taken her back to the basics, she writes, to "nurse the baby, scrub the bathroom, find something to eat. Listen."

In the article "Reflecting Home," in the same issue of *Weavings*, Gerrit Scott Dawson, a Presbyterian minister, notes the importance of building a home as a gathering place, "ordered by love and filled with constant effort." The father of teenage children, he also observes how the occupants are often less than appreciative. "We love," he writes, "in a million mundane ways." In doing so, we instill the "welcoming love of Christ inside each member."

I've lost track of the number of times Ron and I have watched the 1989 film *Parenthood*. This story of a large ex-tended family is a hilarious and touching portrayal of the anxieties of parents who want the best for their children but are sometimes stymied by how to provide it. Gil, the father of three young children, is beset with anxiety and tries his best to be a good father while also holding a stressful and demanding job. Having received little direction or modeling in this regard from his own father, he is often plagued with self-doubts. His father, in the meantime, is trying to deal with his youngest son, Larry, who shows up at his door with a huge gambling debt and a young son none of the family knew about. Going to Gil with his concerns, the older father laments the long-term vigilance that is part of parenthood. "There is no end zone," he says. "You never cross the finish line, spike the ball, and do your touchdown dance. It never, ever ends."

I am paraphrasing the exact conversation, but the scene never ceases to make me laugh—and then to sigh. With my children now well into adulthood, I understand the never-ending part of vigilance. Hearing an adult child sob over the phone about the death of her beloved dog is as gut-wrenching as recalling her tears over a friend's snubs when she was in kindergarten. The parent's heart requires a unique capacity for endurance and for making the mundane into something truly sacred.

Parental Peer Pressure

Looking back, I am glad I set aside the BH&G book. Down syndrome, in a sense, let me off the hook when it came to having the "perfect" child or being the ideal mother. While I was unsure how Jenny's development would progress, so were those around me. Thus, I was spared the kind of parental peer pressure that besets many mothers and fathers today. This isn't to say it didn't creep up on me later. Eric and Anna each went through phases of childhood and adolescence that threw me into doubt about my parenting abilities. The thought that others were observing my massive mistakes was unsettling. Thus, I am ever-grateful to Eric for once telling me, "If I ever go into therapy, I won't blame you."

The anxiety level among parents might be at an all-time high in this age of television reality and talk shows as well as access to instant news via the Internet and social media. I recall, for example, the afternoon of the terrible shootings at Columbine High School in Littleton, Colorado. While students were still streaming out of the building in a panic, newscasters were ruminating about the shooters and what kind of parents they must have. This rush to judgment around the parents' role in a child's violent acts is distressing and unfair. Children will go astray, to be sure, and parents have varying parts to play in such situations. Holding ourselves accountable for a child's well-being is an essential part of self-vigilance.

There are limits to what we can do, however. No matter what messages are given through the media, it's important to remember that children are not a reflection of us. Each one is an individual. Holding the tension between protecting a child enough to feel safe and secure and allowing him or her increasing levels of independence is a delicate balancing act. Helicopter parenting constricts their growth and tethers them to a parent's aspirations. Parental peer pressure ties a parent to a child's behavior and proffers the illusion that parents are or should be in absolute control of their children's lives. A critical task of parenthood is raising children to be self-defined. While parents teach and model for them, in the end they are responsible for who they are and what they do. The vigilance involved in parenting requires letting go in slow but steady ways so that children grow up to be responsible, loving, caring, and compassionate adults. Lots of "bending over" is required between those first steps, however, and the ones that lead out into the world. None of it is meant to be attempted on one's own.

Vigilant Companions

A saving grace for Gayle Boss turned out to be a Friday morning playgroup that provided "socialization opportunities" for young children. In truth, Boss and the other mothers found the greatest amount of socialization with one another. She found in these companions "a sisterhood of women wounded in our self-confidence and uncertain of our worth and identity in a land that offered us no rewards other than lip service."

Boss' experience is not unique. A number of young moms groups around the country provide a vital form of mutual support and encouragement. My own work as a spiritual director and public speaker gives me the opportunity to direct retreats and hold conversations with some of these groups. Each time, I am touched by the way the mothers care for one another. Some live in neighborhoods where other households are empty during the day because the occupants are at work. It leaves these women lonely and isolated. Others hold full- or part-time jobs outside of the home and struggle to find a balance between the two. Still others are raising a child on their own, caring for a child with special needs, or dealing with stressful circumstances in their family. Whenever I gather with a group like this, the tears as well as the laughter flow freely. They truly know what it's like to walk in another mother's shoes.

A father's companions are more likely to be one-on-one friendships rather than groups. With the rise in the number of stay-at-home dads, however, this is also changing. Online support systems are cropping up, thus offering fathers another way to connect with one another. However it is found, the chance to talk to other fathers provides a way to maintain and strengthen the vigilant heart. For both mothers and fathers, the need to connect with other parents for companionship, information, caring, and support is crucial.

The Gift of Patience

Hal Walter is a pack burro racer from Colorado who became a father later in life. As a stay-at-home dad, he cares for his autistic son on a day-to-day basis. During an interview on the radio program "Colorado Matters," Walter told how he never expected to be a father let alone deal with autism. Though noting that the experiences are wildly different, he draws a parallel between dealing with the varying temperaments of the pack burros he races up mountain passes and the day-to-day care of an autistic child. Both burro and child require extreme patience in order to allow them to go their own way. In his book *Full Tilt Boogie*, he writes, "It's how you handle what happens and go with the flow that determines success, whether that means winning or merely finishing some days. That's how life works, too." All one can do is wait and see.

I wonder how much time I spent in waiting rooms at the orthodontist or waiting for a temper tantrum to end, the eye-rolling to be outgrown, or the Christmas holiday that would bring my children back home. There is no way to remain vigilant without the gift of patience. Check a thesaurus, and the word "vigilance" is equated with endurance, tolerance, persistence, stamina, and unflappability. My favorite is "staying power." It affirms a biblical sense of patience that is rooted in trust and hope. "Wait for the LORD; be strong and let your heart take courage; wait for the LORD!" (Psalm 27:14). That might just be one of the most perfect prayers a parent can ever utter.

The gift of patience is certainly needed with children, but it's also needed with ourselves. Since there is no basic training for parenthood, we must learn as we go. The root of the word "courage" comes from the Latin *cor*, which means heart. Francis de Sales noted the importance of courage in maintaining a healthy sense of our own limitations. "Have patience with all things, but chiefly have patience with yourself. Do not lose courage in considering your own imperfections but instantly set about remedying them—every day begin the task anew." Along with patience, then, comes an ability to forgive ourselves for being less than perfect. It also takes waiting upon God to show us the way forward.

The biblical characters described earlier in this chapter certainly exemplified what this means. Abraham and Sarah, Hannah, and Elizabeth and Zechariah are models of patience as they await the movement of God in their lives. Those longing for children through pregnancy or adoption can certainly relate to the "staying power" these figures had while also holding onto hope. It makes the old saying "patience is a virtue" all the more relevant.

Mary, on the other hand, was young and certainly not expecting to become a mother prior to her marriage to Joseph. The "yes" she gave to God at the time of the Annunciation was not just once and for all. It bore repeating throughout the arc of her life—from the visitation of an angel while she was a teenager to the wizened woman who sat among the disciples at Pentecost. In between those two events, how many times did she draw upon the reserves of her spirit to summon the patience needed to follow the path chosen for her? Prayer had to have been woven in and out of each experience.

Prayer for the Present Moment

Prayer is vital to all states of the heart. In order to maintain a vigilant heart, however, the practice of contemplation is particularly vital. Contemplative prayer is not something attainable only by monks and nuns but weaves itself into everyday experiences and the rhythm, however chaotic, of family life. The Jesuit theologian Walter Burghardt called it "a long, loving look at the real." Thomas Merton described it as a "loving sense of this life and this presence and this eternity." Both descriptions make it ideal for cultivating a heart of vigilance. It sharpens our attention to where we are and what we are doing. As such, contemplation provides a way to pray without words or particular formulas, opening our heart to see beyond the mundane. It's a prayer for the present moment.

Contemplative practice also teaches the importance of surrender. This is no easy task in a culture that values independence and promotes the illusion that we can maintain absolute control over everything that happens to us. Mary's response to the angel Gabriel is a huge contrast to such a mindset. "Here I am, the servant of the Lord; let it be with me according to your word" (Luke 1:38).

I, for one, have a very hard time with this kind of response, since I often have such great advice to give God about my family. Sitting by Jenny's bedside during the early days of her life taught me a critical lesson, however. Our children are not our possessions. The best we can do—and I do mean the *very best*—is give them over to God and ask for the kind of wisdom, understanding, grace, and patience we need to guide them toward adulthood. Rather than mere passivity, however, such a stance places us in the spaciousness of God's heart. Catherine of Siena described patience as "the very marrow of love." Waiting upon God opens the heart and invites us to relax into our role as parents.

Tending the Vigilant Heart

Our youngest child, Anna, came along in unexpected fashion. I didn't realize I was pregnant right away because nursing Jenny and then Eric had interrupted my menstrual cycle. As a result, it was difficult to predict an actual due date. This made each day of my pregnancy, especially toward the end, a process of heightened vigilance. Anna was born with her eyes wide open, something the doctor said is a rare occurrence. From the moment she entered the world, Anna had a gift for being in the present moment. She's taught me a great deal about this over the years.

When it comes to practicing vigilance, little children can be the best instructors. They are ever aware of their surroundings, and they are great practitioners of what Brother Lawrence, a seventeenth-century friar, called "little interior glances." Gerald May describes these as "simple things: unadorned

remembrances…happening within the ordinary activities of
our lives. They come and go. They are not to be held on to"
(*The Awakened Heart*). Given all the distractions, anxieties,
fears, and details that beset a parent on any given day, being
drawn back to the present moment is critical. It not only
builds a routine of ongoing prayer, but also offers a way to
counter some of the challenges to vigilance.

Dealing with the mundane is one of them. Without a
vigilant heart, parents can veer in two opposing directions,
each one a threat to a healthy spirituality. One is drifting—a
perpetual restlessness and inability to anchor oneself any-
where. Such a tendency not only keeps the parent in a state
of endless dissatisfaction but also puts the rest of the family
on edge. The other is entrenching and making routines so
sacrosanct that any deviance is met with intransigence. David
Steindl-Rast, author of the book *Common Sense Spirituality*,
describes both tendencies as well-disguised forms of fear. "We
fear to be still, and we fear to be 'still moving.'" Once we are
aware of the tendency we are drawn toward, however, we can
take steps to resist it and open our hearts to the now. Other
parents who understand what we are experiencing help to
keep us on track.

It is also important to retain interest in things away from
and outside of the home. After all, we had a life before children and will have one after they leave home. Having a life
while they are still growing is a necessity. I learned a valuable
lesson about this from my mother. While raising six children,
she was also involved in a number of activities and organi-
zations. Once a week she served as a volunteer at a local hospital. She attended monthly gatherings of the Sacred Heart

Alumnae—women who attended schools run by the Sisters of the Society of the Sacred Heart. I was always taken with the intelligence of these women and how they used their monthly gatherings to not only socialize but also to plan outreach to the poor and to grow more deeply in their faith. Their meetings generally included a guest speaker, and their chaplain, a Jesuit priest, kept them abreast of the changes happening in the Catholic Church as a result of the Second Vatican Council. They modeled for me the importance of growing in faith as adults.

For parents in circumstances that preclude such activities and limit involvement in outside activities, there are still a number of ways to stay active and engaged. Reading, watching uplifting films and documentaries, listening to podcasts that inform and inspire—all are great ways to feed the mind and heart.

Another threat to vigilance is parental pressure that ramps up the "deadly Cs" of parenthood: comparison, competition, and criticism. Each one does damage to the heart by putting us on a fast track toward false standards of perfectionism. We can counter each by making an intentional effort to move in more positive directions.

FROM COMPARISON TO ACCEPTANCE

Accepting ourselves as we are moves us to let go of the "never enough" syndrome, one that keeps us perpetually dissatisfied and tempted to drift. Each of us is gifted, but as Paul reminds us, our gifts are not identical. For example, I never did have the gift for making our house the hub of the neighborhood and hosting the extemporaneous meals that characterized the homes of our children's friends. What I was able to do, however, was create memorable experiences more suited to our more introverted natures. Ron and I relished smaller gatherings over large ones and brought our children to quiet places in nature that created some of our most cherished family memories. Discernment of a parent's gifts doesn't need to be complicated and involved. Instead, it might entail reflection on a few simple questions. What do I have the heart for? Where do my daydreams take me? What ignites my passion? Follow the trail, and the gifts will open up.

FROM COMPETITION TO COMPASSION

Women have a great capacity to gather and support one another in times of need. Nowhere does this surface more strongly than among mothers. Consider groups like Mothers Against Drunk Driving (MADD), for example, or the original intent of Mother's Day as a day of peace supported by and for mothers around the world. These were movements of solidarity. Nevertheless, there is a lot of competition bred into women—competing over men, for example, or using our children to prove how good, capable, and competent we are. Fathers are likewise prone to competition, particularly in the areas of sports and business. Competing for the "most perfect parent" award devalues those we love as well as ourselves. Try to imagine Mary and Elizabeth stressing over who is the better mother, or Joseph and Zechariah squaring off in a contest to prove who was the more faithful and long-suffering spouse. Each one faced enormous challenges as a parent and as a woman or man. Elizabeth probably experienced years of shame over her inability to have children.

Mary faced humiliation and even death for being pregnant outside of marriage. Joseph and Zechariah had their own share of perplexity over circumstances that were completely out of their control. Each one emerges in the gospels as a figure of compassion. This is extended not only to others but also to themselves as they accept their circumstances with humility and remain vigilant to the presence of God in their lives.

Parenting offers a marvelous opportunity to grow more deeply as compassionate people. In my own life, having a child with special needs broke open the reality of the kind of parenting Hal Walter and many others provide each day for their children. In like manner, sitting by a sick baby's bedside made me all the more attentive to the pain of those who ache with and for their children. Compassion for families suffering from poverty, hunger, disease, exile, estrangement, and other maladies of body and soul breaks down tendencies to compete and compare ourselves to others. In the end, we humbly admit we are doing the best we can.

FROM CRITICISM TO SELF-LOVE

"Monkey mind" is the habit of picking at ourselves through criticism and negative self-talk. It can entail overthinking things to the point of mental exhaustion or second-guessing decisions until we back ourselves into a corner of continual self-reproach. Needless to say, it's not a healthy state of the heart. The antidote is learning to love ourselves.

Self-love is not a process of continually patting ourselves on the back or an exercise in narcissism. Instead, it simply embraces who we are and recognizes our own needs. A vigilant heart enables us to deal with our own failings with grace and good humor. By letting go of unreal expectations around perfection and by loving ourselves for who we are, we learn a great lesson about doing the same for our children.

In order to move from monkey mind to tender heart, we also need moments of respite in order to step back and take stock of our lives and circumstances, to breathe deeply and cut ourselves some slack. This allows a spaciousness of heart in which love for God, for others, and for ourselves grows more abundantly. One of the greatest practitioners of self-love was Jesus. While his public ministry had him on the go, with people crying out for his attention and healing on a non-stop basis, he took regular time-outs—for prayer and reflection as well as to be with family and friends. He is a reminder of the need to care for ourselves as tenderly as we do our children. Doing so opens up another state of the heart—that of joy.

Questions *for* Reflection *and* Discussion

Why is vigilance such an important part of parenting? How does it change in light of different stages in the life of the family or in the circumstances of a parent (single parent, stepparent, adoptive parent, etc.)?

Adult "peer pressure" is one form of stress for parents. What other pressures do parents face?

In addition to patience, what other gifts do parents need to maintain a vigilant heart?

TWO

The JOYFUL HEART

THERE ARE A LOT OF "FIRSTS" ASSOCIATED WITH MY CHILDREN'S GROWTH: FIRST SMILE, FIRST WORD, FIRST DAY OF SCHOOL...The watching and waiting that was part of vigilance opened into joy as they acquired a new ability or made a new discovery. Sometimes these experiences came with mixed emotions. Watching them learn to read is a case in point. It was magical to see them decipher the words on the page and then piece together entire stories. Once they could immerse themselves in their own books, however, their interest in reading together diminished. I missed the time spent opening up the worlds of Oz or Narnia with them. The same conflicted feelings accompanied the times when we handed over the car keys or watched them pack up for their first foray into a life of independence. It felt as if my heart was bursting open with happiness and pride while also constricting a bit with apprehension and anxiety.

"Joy" isn't a word that generally pops up in day-to-day conversation. Perhaps it's because joy is not nearly as easy to pin down as happiness, cheerfulness, pleasure, and other synonyms. In a spiritual sense, joy runs much deeper. It generates from within rather than from external events or experiences. Thus, it is possible to be joyful within the jumble of emotions that accompany parenting.

One of the most joyful encounters in the Scriptures is the visit Mary pays to her cousin Elizabeth. Two pregnant women meet and greet one another with excitement and enthusiasm. Elizabeth describes the baby "leaping" within her at the sight of her beloved cousin. Mary's song of praise describes the joyful state of her heart and how, in time, "all generations will call me blessed" (Luke 1:48). Each woman is happily anticipating the wonder of giving birth and the grace of watching her child grow, mature, and set off on his own. Their meeting is a reminder of the stages of a child's life—from infant to adult—that are cause for a parent's joy.

In his book *The Holy Longing*, Ronald Rolheiser lists four non-negotiable essentials of Christian spirituality: private prayer and private morality, social justice, community as a constituent element of worship, and mellowness of heart and spirit. The last one is particularly striking. It counters the association made between spirituality and rigorous ascetics or somber practices. As Philip Neri observed, "There is no such thing as a sad saint."

While parenting entails serious responsibility, it also encompasses moments of unbridled joy. In preparing to write this chapter, I asked a number of friends and acquaintances to describe some of the joys they experience as parents. Their responses ran along a similar line. Author Dolores Curran summed it up best by distinguishing between the "pleasures of parenting" and its joys. "Pleasure includes daily activities like youth sports, having fun with our children, celebrating their achievements and so forth. Joy touches the heart when we witness and oversee the development of these unique individuals sent to us by God: overcoming childhood fears, showing concern for siblings, exhibiting unexpected generosity, and offering spontaneous expressions of gratitude and love." She then noted the small but meaningful expressions of gratefulness, such as "I'm glad you're my mother," and "I'm lucky to have you for my dad." Each one "plants a joyful legacy in any parent's heart."[1]

There are different ways in which such a legacy builds over the years. Four in particular, however, are well-suited for deepening the spirituality of parents. These are delight, wonder, gratitude, and love.

Joy as Delight

My maternal grandmother had seven children. She used to say she wished they all were twins. I don't think there was any way she could have envisioned such a large brood without the levity that permeated her family. My mother, in turn,

---

1.   I am grateful to Dolores for giving me permission to quote and edit her words, sent to me in an e-mail.

brought this lightheartedness into our home. Whenever I gather with my five siblings, the laughter flows freely as we recall the experience of growing up in our large and boisterous family. My father's side of the family was more somber. Even so, my father was quite expressive about the delight he took in our family. This increased as he approached the end of his life. On the occasion of our last gathering with him, I recall how the entire family—children, in-laws, grandchildren, and pets—drew around him. While he knew many satisfying moments in his long career as a businessman, being parent and grandparent was his true delight. It brought a mellowness of heart like nothing else could.

Ron and I too found moments of great delight in raising our children. Watching Jenny play with the junk mail—one of her favorite pastimes—was just one of the simple pleasures we took in seeing her regain her strength and stamina after surgery. Eric seemed to have an "old soul" from the time he was a toddler and never ceased to surprise us with some of his observations about the world. Anna was such a sweet and happy baby that I was stopped repeatedly in the grocery store so people could revel in her smile. When Anna would accuse Eric of being a "slow pope" or Eric, at the ripe old age of five, asked if we ever thought about the meaning of life, the words quickly made their way to my journal. Savoring and then recording their observations made for wonderful moments of levity and delight.

While there is a certain amount of anxiety involved in the vigilant heart, it is offset by the sheer joy of watching children grow and develop. My friend Barbara brought this to mind when I discussed with her the writing of this book.

Although not a parent herself, she finds great joy in her relationship with her nephew. In an e-mail she told how she visits with him every Friday morning. "It's a joy especially because I have not spent much time with him since he was a little boy. I find it is so delightful when I learn something from him." She went onto describe how he brings insights that both engage and enlighten her. "Do parents feel the same way?" she asked.

In the last chapter I noted how children are not reflections of their parents. This makes for some of the most delightful experiences of parenting. Even as babies, children display a personality that is wholly her or his own. Just as identical twins have their own set of fingerprints, so does every child have a particular character. Watching this emerge is a fascinating process.

I admit that I sometimes have to laugh when reading the rapturous writings of new parents or quotes from celebrities who have just discovered the joy of parenting. Usually these observations are written about infants and toddlers. Parents who are farther along in the process know that once children enter adolescence the sweet smells and cute sayings quickly dissipate. Nonetheless, another kind of delight takes hold. Teenagers have their own humorous observations about life, along with interesting insights about the issues they and their peers face. They can surprise us with their capacity for empathy and generosity. Sometimes the delight lies simply in the fact that they survived this period of life and the parent made it through those years with their mental faculties intact. My own parents had six children born over a span of twenty years. This means they had teenagers in the house for over two decades! The delight my father took in his family over the course of his life illustrates how joy deepens over time and how it is rooted in wonder.

Joy as Wonder

The intersection of joy with wonder gives rise to deeper awareness about the grace of God enfolded into all life. In Luke's gospel, Mary made such a connection in her lovely prayer of joy. No one taught me a greater lesson about this than Jenny. As our first child, she introduced me to the joy of parenting through the experience of pregnancy and childbirth. Since we knew nothing about Down syndrome, Ron and I had little choice but to remain open to life. I believe this experience, in turn, opened us further to the wonder of human growth and development.

In the many responses I received about the joy of parenting, no one noted how satisfying it was to see their children become replicas of themselves. Instead, each parent reveled in the unique individuality of a child. Watching children mature through even the difficult, obnoxious, and puzzling stages is a true wonder. Their individuality emerges and blossoms. They sometimes take us by surprise with their insights and observations. In addition, they draw something unexpected out of us as parents.

On the online blog *On Being*, John Cary described how he discovered his natural gift of creativity with the birth of his daughter. Entrapped by a deadening job, he feared that too much energy was being drained away from his family. Taking photographs of his daughter drew out his playful nature. It started right after she was born when he placed her tightly swaddled body on a bed covered with paper name tags. Writing her name on one, he placed it on her chest and then used the photo as a birth announcement. As his little girl grew, she began to take a more active role in the father-daughter photos. They dressed in identical costumes for some and staged hilarious scenarios in others. Describing the awakening that arose with the experience of fatherhood, he writes, "I knew from that moment forward that the person I wanted and needed to be as a father—creative, emotional, vulnerable— was the opposite of the person that I felt like in my job. One of those things had to go, and ultimately did" ("Becoming a Father Restored My Creativity," John Cary, www.onbeing. org/blog/becoming-a-father-restored-my-creativity/7685). Cary's story epitomizes the transformative potential within parenting and how it leads us to decisions that are far better for our hearts and souls. The most natural reaction to such transformation is gratitude.

Joy as Gratitude

Author Anne Lamott writes that her two favorite prayers are, "Help me, help me, help me" and "Thank you, thank you, thank you." I certainly expressed both as we awaited the outcome of Jenny's surgery. Once she was released from the hospital and our lives took on a more normal routine, I knew the deep gratitude that arises after making it through a trying experience.

Gratitude is not hard to put into practice when emerging from a heartrending situation. The relief one feels when a child recovers from an illness or finds his or her way home after a period of alienation evokes prayers of thanksgiving in easy fashion. Making gratitude a daily practice takes more time and intention. Parents, however, have a hundred different reasons to give thanks throughout the day.

Lamott's "thank you, thank you, thank you" prayer may be all a busy parent can muster when climbing into bed at night after carting a vanload of children to soccer practice or spending the day caring for a sick child. In regularly pausing to reflect upon and express our thanks, we reap the benefits of gratitude. David Steindl-Rast heads the Network for Grateful Living, an organization dedicated to cultivating gratitude. He describes its benefits this way: "I'm not grateful because I'm happy; I'm happy because I'm grateful." A regular practice of gratitude gives rise to more positive thinking and strengthens resilience, coping skills, and a more balanced approach to life. When observing something within the moment for which to be grateful—whether it's keeping up with the boundless energy of a ten-year-old or rocking a colicky baby back to sleep—the heart softens and yields to the joy of being wrapped in God's care. Often this is only recognized in hindsight.

The joy of parents whose children have reached adulthood offers an insight into the wonder of parenting over the long haul. My friend Jim describes the way in which he watched his son and daughter each struggle with life decisions and then learn from their choices. "My heart is filled with the peace of mind that they will be okay, especially with the help of God." Another friend, Vickie, echoes a similar sentiment in an e-mail about her children. "We will always be their parents," she writes, "but now we are also their companions in their life journey on a different level. The biggest joy now is that we continue to share in the joys and struggles of their lives and the parenting of their own children." The gratitude in each of these accounts illustrates a heart expanding in love.

Joy as Love

In her book *Grace (Eventually)*, Anne Lamott describes the anxiety she faced as a single mother with limited financial resources. "My faith told me that my child and I would be covered, that God's love, as expressed in the love of my friends and family, would provide for us one hundred percent of the time. This turned out to be true..." No matter what the circumstances, most parents can look back on their experience of parenting with wonder at how things worked out—the extra money that came in time to stretch the household budget, the crisis that turned out to be a blessing in disguise, the unanticipated words of wisdom that sprang to the lips in order to soothe a child's woes. None of it is magical, but it is often mysterious. As it did with Lamott, the love of family, friends, members of a faith community, and others can sustain us during some of the most trying times, encourage us during mundane moments, and revel with us in the large and small reasons for celebration.

Parenting is like a continuous treasure hunt in which one keeps uncovering more gifts and surprises. It awakens a recognition of God's expansive heart and our immersion in it. Gerald May describes love as less of a *function* and more of a *capacity*. This implies spaciousness and a heart flexible enough to expand. "It is out of the pristine ground of the heart that true assent and fidelity must finally come, stripped of external justifications and rational explanation" (*The Awakened Heart*). One of the great wonders of such spaciousness is discovering how much love we are capable of giving. There is a scary element to this, to be sure. The image of the heart "walking around outside the body" keeps it exposed and vulnerable. Even so, the experience of parenting can teach more than a thousand books can about what it means to give and receive love as well as to hold faith in God, whose love is everlasting.

Joyful Companions

One of the most endearing aspects of the encounter between Mary and Elizabeth is the span in their ages. Elizabeth is an older woman, well past childbearing age, who finds herself on the brink of something truly mystifying. Mary is a teenager and, as such, is just starting what will be a long and emotionally charged experience of motherhood. They stay together for an entire trimester. Luke doesn't offer many details about their visit. Even so, it's not hard to imagine the support and encouragement they gave one another, as well as the laughter they shared as they wove baby blankets and talked about their plans for the months and years to come.

Cross-generational bonds are a true gift to parents no matter what the age or stage of their children. I saw how this works while directing a mothers' retreat a few years ago. The topic was the spirituality of time. After giving a presentation about the importance of taking time each day for reflection and quiet, a group of younger women had a meltdown. One of them announced loudly that, as a "Type A" personality, her responsibilities as a mother wouldn't allow for such an indulgence. Before I could respond, a number of the older women calmed everyone down. They encouraged the younger women to let go of the "small stuff" and to simply enjoy the time they now had with their children.

The need for cross-generational support is as important for fathers as it is for mothers. Older people, particularly grandparents or wizened figures in the parish or neighborhood, hold a "long view" and thus provide perspective and offer experiences to inspire and encourage younger parents. In exchange, younger parents have a fresh perspective on their role in an ever-changing world. I recall, for example, how much my father admired Ron for the way in which he was involved with the day-to-day care of our children. As a stay-at-home dad, Ron experienced fatherhood in a way previous generations had not. Such admiration marked the responses about joy that I received from many empty-nest parents. They watch their children become parents and tackle life's challenges with tremendous admiration and respect.

Gifts for Joy

Whenever I read the account of Elizabeth in Luke's gospel, I think that Zechariah was given a great gift when he was struck with an inability to speak. It might have been his best option around a wife who was both menopausal and pregnant! Perhaps his involuntary silence allowed him to appreciate his experience with a lighter heart since he couldn't explain anything to anyone.

My sister Corinne is a true inspiration to me. While not a great deal older than me, she has nevertheless modeled the humor a parent needs to maintain a joyful heart. As the mother of five daughters, four now with children of their own, she has been through many parental ups and downs.

Over the years she has retained a wonderful ability to laugh freely and abundantly. Corinne might be seen by others as someone with little to laugh about. Weakened and in pain as a result of myositis and acute arthritis, she could easily slip into self-pity. Instead, she attends a laugh therapy session each week as a way to maintain high spirits and lighten her heart. Her family offers plenty of material to take to these sessions.

In addition to adding levity to our lives, humor enlarges the heart's capacity for love. Even when laden with difficulties, there is plenty of joy within the adventure of parenting. The delight, wonder, gratitude, and love folded into the experience gives rise to laughter and mirth, particularly when we are tempted to take ourselves too seriously. The late humorist and author Erma Bombeck taught this lesson beautifully. Not only was she able to poke fun at her less-than-perfect housekeeping abilities, but she also offered an out for parents who held themselves to unrealistic expectations. She had an eloquent style that tapped into the parent's heart for compassion. In her article "My Favorite Child," she wrote about the way in which the heart opens to the child most in need at the moment, the one "who needs you for whatever reason—to cling to, to shout at, to hurt, to hug, to flatter, to reverse charges to, to unload on—but mostly just to be there."

Prayer to Lift the Heart

In a vein similar to Bombeck, Anne Lamott draws out the importance of prayer that revels in God's grace. In addition to the "help" and "thank you" prayers, she describes "wow" prayers as those arising from wonder and rooted in joy. Such prayer is an amalgam of praise, adoration, and thankfulness that realigns our perceptions and widens our vistas. "Wonder takes our breath away, and makes room for new breath. That's why they call it breathtaking" (*Help, Thanks, Wow*).

Parenthood brings with it a host of reasons to pray with awe. Counting a newborn's fingers and toes and smelling the sweetness emanating from the nape of her neck are among the first. Pile on the moments of relief, pride, admiration, endearment, and hilarity, and the "oh wows" keep coming. Prayers of reverence and awe also offer a blessed respite from the culture's bent toward cynicism and dark, ugly humor that beats down the spirit. Delight, wonder, and gratitude arise in their place, making us all the more aware of God's presence.

Tending the Joyful Heart

John Cary discovered his own creativity as he staged photos with his young daughter. In doing so he found a spiritual wellspring of joy. Some of his photos were included with his blog post and were nothing short of hilarious. In one, he sits in an ice chest with a party hat on his head and an apple in his mouth while his daughter peers at him through a camera set on a tripod. In another the two of them are dressed in identical Evel Knievel outfits. In each picture, the joy of parenting makes itself apparent.

When naming spirituality's most important attributes, I don't suppose hilarity, as we usually think of the word, crops up on many lists. Nevertheless, in his letter to the Romans, Paul does use the Greek word that our word "hilarity" comes from when he encourages his readers to show mercy in "cheerfulness" (Romans 12:8). He uses the word *hilarotes*, which also describes an ever-increasing appreciation for God's endless gifts. Think of a cheerful person in your life. Isn't he or she someone who embraces life with delight, wonder, gratitude, and love? These aspects of joy make the role of a parent all the more lighthearted. Like John Cary, we begin to tap into our own creativity as we make the most of each moment with our children.

This may seem unrealistic when the family schedule is on overload and the laundry is piling up. Some parents work more than one job or commute long distances to work. Others feel isolated and unsupported. Financial resources might be stretched thin, generating stress and anxiety about how to make ends meet. The "sandwich" generation provides caregiving at two levels—for children as well as aging parents. How does one retain a joyful heart in the midst of such challenges? The answer lies in one simple word: sabbath.

"Keeping the sabbath" is the only one of the Ten Commandments starting with the word "remember." In his book *Learning to Pray*, Wayne Muller describes sabbath as a "way of being in time where we remember who we are, remember what we know and taste the gifts of spirit and eternity." In the Bible, this great gift was given to the Israelites after their release from slavery. Imagine what it was like to not only step away from such a life, but also to be given a full day every week to simply enjoy life.

In bestowing the "day of rest" on the Israelites, God invited them to step aside from daily concerns as well as labor, to remember how they are loved and cared for through God's infinite grace and mercy, and to take delight in the world God made and the wonders a single day has to hold. It's well past time that we reclaim this ancient practice. By that I mean more than just showing up for church on Sunday. The latter is certainly an important part of sabbath-keeping, but it requires active participation. Through the celebration of the Eucharist, we are nourished and blessed, joined with our family in faith, and sustained by our communal prayers and rituals.

Once we are drawn into this awareness, we understand sabbath as a space for rest, rejuvenation, refreshment, and renewal. One key way to do this is by managing the use of technology. In his book *Hamlet's Blackberry*, William Powers provides a fascinating look at the evolution of technological advances over the centuries and how each one created a sea-change in human interaction. Having reached the digital age, we are in a relatively new period of technological advancement. This requires navigating our way through devices that can consume vast amounts of time. Powers isn't suggesting they be ditched. Instead, he notes the need for good management of these tools and the importance of finding "gaps" in our lives. Otherwise, our capacity for face-to-face interaction erodes. This has an especially devastating impact on the family.

While parents may be cognizant of the need for parameters around their child's "screen time," they may not be so good at practicing what they preach. "A family isn't a spectator sport," Powers writes. "It's all about participation, engagement, connection of the most intimate kind. At our screens, we're all facing outwards." This realization led him and his wife to set aside one day a week to "unplug." This was as much a challenge for them as it was for their children. What they discovered through the experience, however, was the delight of one another's company and the opportunities to engage in non-screen activities such as reading, hiking, conversing, and sharing meals together. In essence, they discovered a kind of sabbath.

Over the years, Anna has taught me great lessons about finding sabbath time in the midst of ordinary days. As a little girl, she reveled in every chance to do something fun, especially if it involved food. I recall once running errands with her and giving her the chance to pick a place for lunch. "Let's see," she said. "There's Dairy Queen, McDonalds, Burger King... So many good places to eat!" As an adult, her culinary tastes have sharpened, but her delight in finding places to explore never diminished. She is, in some regards, our family "cruise director." It's because of her efforts that I donned a wet suit and dove into a Florida river in order to swim with manatees, boarded a tour boat to watch for whales in Puget Sound, and stood still on the moving walkway at O'Hare Airport just to watch the colors change in the passageway between concourses. Each experience brought an immersion into delight, wonder, and gratitude at the abundance of God's great gifts.

The "gaps" that Powers identifies in his book are essentially little sabbath spaces, ones that keep us alert to the delightful presence of God in our lives. In her book *Time Management for Unmanageable People*, Ann McGee-Cooper calls them "joy breaks." They serve no purpose other than to feed the soul. All parents need them, no matter what the circumstances. They can be as extensive as going on a weekend retreat or as simple as walking around the block. Once we start to make these a regular part of our lives, we remember what it feels like to reclaim the joy of life. In doing so, we find the resilience needed to weather the times when the heart is heavy with grief, worry, and fear.

QUESTIONS *for* REFLECTION *and* DISCUSSION

What particular joys do you experience as a parent or do you witness in the parents you know?

What other gifts, in addition to a sense of humor, increase a parent's capacity for joy?

What kinds of sabbath time might a parent make in his or her life to maintain a joyful heart?

THREE

The HEAVY HEART

SEVERAL YEARS AGO, AS PART OF A PRESENTATION TO A GROUP OF PARENTS, I READ ALOUD A CHILDREN'S BOOK CALLED *THE HURT* BY TEDDI DOLESKI TO DRAW THE TOPIC OF FORGIVENESS INTO A FAMILY CONTEXT. It is the story of a little boy named Justin who nurses a hurt after being called a name by a playmate. Instead of talking to anyone about it, he takes the hurt to his room and feeds it all of his wounded feelings. The hurt grows so large it takes up all the space. Justin finally goes to his father, who gives him sage advice: "When you are ready to let it go, it will leave."

Halfway through the story I noticed a frowning man in the back row. I took his expression to mean either boredom with the presentation or annoyance at being read a children's story. I expected the worst when he approached me at the break. Instead, he asked for the name of the book. "My little boy is hurting over something," he told me, "and I don't know how to help him talk about it. Perhaps this book will help." What I took for a scowl was simply a manifestation of the heavy heart he carried over the hurt in his son's life.

The parent's heart can weigh heavily with many things. When I direct retreats for young mothers, for example, the tears flow freely as they share their anxieties about not being "good enough" mothers and for their children's well-being and safety. Living, as I do, in Colorado, where there have been three shooting incidents in schools and one in a movie theater, such fears are understandable. There are multiple joys connected with parenting, but there is much heartache as well.

The Broken Heart

The prophet Simeon gives some of the most disturbing news a parent could receive when he meets Mary and Joseph in the Temple. "Then Simeon blessed them and said to his mother Mary, 'This child is destined for the falling and rising of many in Israel, and to be a sign that will be opposed, so that the inner thoughts of many will be revealed—and a sword will pierce your own soul too'" (Luke 2:34–35). Imagine the anxiety this triggered in such a young mother. Move farther into the gospels, and we read of this brokenhearted woman standing helplessly at the foot of the cross watching her son die in agony. Other sorrows beset Mary before this—the terrifying flight into Egypt to escape the horror of infanticide; the frantic backtracking to Jerusalem in search of her twelve-year-old son; the betrayal of friends, neighbors, and relatives when Jesus is driven out of her hometown; and her fears for his safety as his teaching became more threatening to religious leaders. Over the course of her life, how often did Mary revisit the prophecy of Simeon and feel the increasing heaviness of her own heart?

Mary's heartbreak became much clearer to me when I experienced my own. After months of relative calm in our lives, I brought Jenny back to the hospital in Denver for surgery to close the colostomy. Things began to go awry when she developed an infection that required an additional surgery and then another. Although weakened by the procedures, she recovered enough so that we could return to Ron (who was unable to take more leave from the Coast Guard) and our home in Alaska. Within a few weeks, however, she began to show signs of distress. After we had made several trips to the local hospital, the doctors agreed on the need for additional treatment back in Denver. On the morning of our departure, we found her dead in her crib. Our sweet child lived only a year and eighteen days, but I feel her loss as strongly today as I did thirty-eight years ago.

In her book *Heart: A Natural History of the Heart-Filled Life*, Gail Godwin describes the grief she experienced after her brother's death by suicide. In attempts to console her, people said she would get over it "in time." This is one of those useless platitudes we offer to one another when at a loss for words. Part of the nature of the broken heart is exactly that you *won't* get over it. The pain may not be as sharp as the immediate aftermath of a death or other devastating experience, but the wound remains. "Heartbreak is an invisible affliction. No limp comes with it, no evident scar. No sticker

that guarantees good parking or easy access. The heart is broken all the same. The soul festers. The wound, untreated, can
be terminal" (Thomas Lynch, as quoted in *Heart*).

The parental experience of "walking around with the heart
outside the body" entails a certain acceptance of heartbreak.
The cost of love, particularly that of a parent for a child, is
the heart opened to suffering. During a women's retreat on
the theme of an open heart, I asked the group to name something that breaks the heart. Responses included death of a
loved one, illness, accidents, and breakup of a relationship
through divorce, abandonment, or neglect. One mother described a horrific situation in which a drug-addled intruder
broke into her home and how she managed to wrestle him
outside of the house. The whole thing was witnessed by her
young son. While the mother was grateful for the evasion of
something far worse, she was also clearly wounded by the
incident. "Sometimes I wish I didn't have to care so much,"
she lamented. Others nodded in understanding. While they
would fight to the death for their children, the strain of such
care takes a toll.

Years ago, I came across an article called "The Limits of
Parenting." It lists how we can guide, teach, mentor, and advise
our children, but in the end, we cannot do for them what they
must do for themselves. Thus, while we can tell our children
about the consequences of certain behaviors, we cannot pre-
vent them from making choices that are ultimately self-destructive. We can model compassionate attitudes but cannot
guarantee they will develop generous and loving hearts. We
can teach them prayers and talk to them about God but cannot give them faith. This sobering understanding of paren-

tal limits explains the number of responses I received from parents who reflected on the joy of watching their children emerge into adulthood. Reading between the lines, one can see that such growth was not without its heart-heavy moments. Letting go of our children is a day-by-day process. It mostly happens in small increments and through everyday experiences. Other times, it happens through brutal experiences, such as holding your child's lifeless body in your arms or keeping vigil over a child with mental illness, physical ailments, or emotional distress. The vulnerable state of the heart then becomes a heavy and sometimes staggering burden.

"The Limits of Parenting" lists a number of difficult subjects that must, in time, be broached by parents. In doing so, the parent's heart aches over the necessity of piercing a child's innocence in an effort to further protect him or her from danger. Consider the words of warning we have to give children about untrustworthy strangers or the dangers of drunken driving, sexually transmitted diseases, and date rape. None are easy to talk about and yet become necessary in order to release a child into the world. There are also the realities of human injustice. I remember the day Anna came to me and asked, "Are we white?" My heart sank because I knew her preschool view of life could not last forever. I was a teacher before I was a mother, however, so I followed my instinct by posing another question. "What do you think?" I asked. She placed her arm next to mine and responded, "I think we're kind of peach." The amusement and relief I felt was accompanied by a bit of heartbreak. I knew that someday that question would be about more than skin tone, and I would need to talk to her about the violence and hatred arising out of fear, anger, prejudice, and all the "isms" that infect society.

Fear Factors

As noted in Chapter 1, there is fear folded into parenting with vigilance. It doesn't dissipate as children grow up and leave home; it simply shifts. The father in *Parenthood* described it as a never-ending process of running the ball toward a goal line forever out of one's reach. Parental fear is often driven by the unknowns in life—the "what ifs" that usually crop up in reliable fashion around 3:00 in the morning. This can lead to helicopter parenting in an attempt to shield a child from anything difficult and challenging.

Fear can also be generated by experience or from the narratives we craft about our lives. Deborah Tannen describes some of the latter in her book *You're Wearing That?*, an insightful exploration of the complicated communication patterns that develop between mother and daughter. After conversing with numerous women about the topic, she notes how nearly every mother expressed her fear over not being a "good mother." This reflects some of the anxiety I hear when directing retreats for mothers. Some of it arises from personal experiences of disappointment and failure in a woman's life—worries about how a divorce affected a child, for example, or reactive behaviors stemming back to childhood and a disappointing relationship with one's own mother. Add societal expectations around what constitutes a "good" mother (or father) and the fear ramps up even further. Much of this is a relatively new phenomenon. I can't imagine my own mother, for example, stressing about how I perceived her offhanded comments. My peers, however, have a different experience. Every mother I know with an adult daughter confesses to a certain amount of self-doubt after conversing over the phone or via e-mail or text messaging. Our concern is that we not be perceived as critical or judgmental. It's a different kind of vigilance that weighs heavily on the heart.

Two Forms of Heartbreak

Writer and educator Parker Palmer describes the "tragic gap" as that which lies between what is and what could be. He notes the need to learn how to hold the tension between the primitive brain and the responsive heart. This leads to true faith and a civilized world. Every religious tradition, he notes, has some kind of belief in the alchemy that can transform suffering into new life. Christian faith in the resurrection embraces the hope that life can emerge from death and that light can break the darkness. One doesn't get to the resurrection, however, without first experiencing the crucifixion. Palmer notes that the only way to make our way across the tragic gap is through a willingness to have our hearts broken. With this, he describes two forms of heartbreak.

THE SHATTERED HEART

The first is the heart broken into shards that we aim at the source of our pain. Palmer describes the shattered heart as an unresolved wound. Like Justin in *The Hurt*, we may hide it and then feed it all of our disappointments, resentments, anger, and slights until it fills up our entire life. Other times we direct the broken shards toward others in a frustrated attempt to resolve the hurt once and for all, or we try to numb the pain with alcohol, food, drugs, or other self-destructive behavior. Far too many adults lack the wisdom Justin showed in seeking his father's help and then letting the hurt go. Instead, we let the wounds fester until they become deadly.

Being on the receiving end of someone's shattered heart is a painful and sometimes dangerous experience. Franciscan priest Richard Rohr sums it up this way: "What we don't transform, we transmit." Consider all of the wounded parents who unconsciously transmit to their children the hurts suffered through the neglect, abuse, or absence of their own parents. It leads to family systems awash in dysfunction and pain.

THE HEART BROKEN OPEN

Palmer describes how the parents of a rebellious teenager demonstrate what it means to stand in the tragic gap. They must hold the tension between the hope they have for their child and the reality of what is happening in that child's life. "If the parents fail to hold that tension, they will go one way or the other, clinging to an idealized fantasy of who 'their baby' is or rejecting this 'thorn in their side' with bitter cynicism" (*A Hidden Wholeness*). Those parents who do manage to hold the tension, however, not only serve their child well; they also open their hearts and become wiser and more compassionate in the process.

An open heart is expanded rather than constricted by pain. This is the essence of the passage from Ezekiel in which the "heart of stone" is removed and replaced by one of flesh. Openheartedness keeps us human, alive, caring, and compassionate in the way of Jesus. Referring to the account of Mary of Bethany who anoints Jesus' feet with precious oil, C.S. Lewis observed: "The precious alabaster box which we have to break open over the holy feet is our heart."

The Openhearted Parent

Palmer's helpful distinction between the two forms of heartbreak make the heavy heart an opportunity for rich spiritual growth. From this vantage point, I can honestly say that Jenny's physical and mental challenges expanded my own heart in ways I could never have imagined. Down syndrome brought a new understanding of the grace enfolded in one of the most challenging experiences of a parent—that of caring for a child with physical, mental, or emotional disabilities. Her surgeries, difficult as they were, made me all the more aware of the suffering of parents who keep vigil by a child's bedside. Her death awakened a depth of compassion and empathy for those who mourn their children's death with cries that rend the heart. And the passage of time has shown me that the broken-open heart, while never fully mended again, yields to a softer and more loving way of seeing and embracing the world. It makes possible an understanding of what it means to find life in the process of losing it.

In another blog posted on the *On Being* website, guest contributor Elizabeth Aquino described the care she gives to her daughter, Sophie, on a 24/7 basis. It is an experience that allows her to hold two seemingly contradictory emotions of joy and sorrow together. "I can look at Sophie and grieve for the loss of 'normalcy,' but I can also exult in her being exactly the way she is. I can have sorrow over the absurdity of changing a near-17-year-old's diapers and marvel at the gift of intimacy that entails…I'm heading toward an under-standing of openness—of what it means to be truly open to experience,…to, dare I say it, love" ("Hanging by a Thread," www.onbeing.org/content/elizabeth-aquino).

One of the most striking things about Aquino's blog post is her realistic view of what she has been dealt. There's no su-garcoating the situation with ridiculous statements like "God won't give me more than I can handle." She doesn't romanti-cize her parenting role nor does she whine about it. In facing the reality of her pain, she acknowledges and moves into it rather than trying to deny or escape it. According to Palmer, this is one way across the tragic gap. Another is by creating a quiet space around ourselves. This allows the turmoil in our lives to settle and an inner quiet to surface. It also gives rise to hidden graces, ones we might miss when wrapped up in frenetic activity or numbed into oblivion. This quiet space makes for a hospitable heart, one that receives not only one's own pain but also that of others.

Openhearted Companions

In 2012, Elizabeth Aquino initiated "The Extreme Parenting Video Project." She asked parents of children and young adults with disabilities for words of encouragement and support. Aquino then invited them to write these messages on poster board and pose for a photo. She compiled the submissions into a beautiful video that was made available online. (The video is still accessible through YouTube.) One of the most frequent messages was about the importance of seeking help. Without support, parenting can be a lonely and isolating job and the heavyhearted experiences even more difficult to bear.

As joyful as it was to welcome Jenny into the world, the news of her Down syndrome wore heavy on the heart. As I noted earlier, the term "mentally challenged" had not yet come into everyday language at the time of her birth. Ron and I had no clue what we were facing, and there were few people around us at that time to help. By God's grace, we ended up in Alaska in a place where there was a strong support system for parents of children with special needs. The subsequent rise in such support is a hopeful development. Some of these are formal groups tailored to a particular parenting situation. Others, like mother's groups or online conversation sites, offer companionship and encouragement. Most of all, they entail mutual understanding.

The Gift of Resilience

Support systems often provide resources that inform and inspire, thus assisting in keeping the heart open and receptive. This makes resilience an important gift for a parent with a heavy heart. Resilience prevents the heart-shattering reactions that wound the parent further as well as those around him or her. I suppose if Ron and I were to choose a motto for the experience of parenting, it would be "hold things loosely." With Jenny's birth, we discovered pretty quickly that children don't come into the world with any sort of playbook. Our other two children only affirmed this understanding.

All parents face this reality. Just when we think we have a handle on a particular stage in a child's life, something shifts. The mellow infant enters the terrible twos; the ever-cheerful child becomes a moody and rebellious teenager; the self-confident young adult enters a mid-life crisis. In the blink of an eye, family situations can change. An accident or illness realigns all priorities; an unexpected pregnancy disrupts the "master plan"; the discovery of a child's learning disabilities generates a new set of challenges. Holding things loosely keeps the heart pliant and the spirit ready to take on the challenges of parenting with grace.

The Prayer of Lament

Several years after Jenny's death, I attended the funeral of a young woman who was killed in a car accident after heading in the wrong direction on the interstate. Alcohol played a part in the crash that ensued, setting the car in which she was riding aflame and making the identification of her body even more difficult. I don't think I have witnessed a more heartbreaking sight than that of her parents following her coffin down the aisle of the church. As if this tragedy wasn't enough, their older son had died a few years before in another highway accident.

I could say I understood their grief because of my own experience with Jenny but, in truth, I could not. Jenny's death was extraordinarily painful and left a hole in my heart that will never completely heal. Her death came after so much surgery, however, that her body was depleted. In some ways, I watched her fade away as her strength ebbed and the shadow of death drew nearer. The randomness of a car accident, however, entails an entirely different kind of grief and pain. Tolstoy described it perfectly when he wrote, "All happy families are alike; each unhappy family is unhappy in its own way" (*Anna Karenina*). Be it death, illness, hunger, poverty, or exile, every parent's pain is unique. Each walk of bereavement, anxiety, and desperation is a long and lonely one.

The beauty and depth of the psalms, particularly those addressing the laments that run deep in human experience, makes them well-suited for the heavy heart. Some are difficult to read, to be sure, unless one has known the same kind of desolation and despair. The psalmists are not afraid to question where God has gone during such times and describe suffering with graphic and heartbreaking images. Take the following example:

> Save me, O God,
> for the waters have come up to my neck.
> I sink in deep mire, where there is no foothold;
> I have come into deep waters,
> and the flood sweeps over me.
> I am weary with my crying;
> my throat is parched.
> My eyes grow dim with waiting for my God.
> *Psalm 69:1–3*

This could be considered a "how long" prayer—how long must I wait for relief, for consolation, for assurance that my suffering will not endure indefinitely? It is the cry of every mother and father who has buried a child, for every child crying out for bread, for every family struggling with the onset of physical or mental illness in one of its members. The prayer of lament actually takes a great deal of faith—faith in a God who may seem silent but who waits for us with a merciful and open heart.

Conflicts and the Heart

It would not be realistic to write a book about the spirituality of parenting without mentioning experiences of alienation and conflict. Sometimes, despite our best efforts, children rebel and run away from home and all the love we try to give them. The parable of the prodigal son (Luke 15:11–32) describes such a situation in a way that remains relevant to this day. In his book *The Return of the Prodigal Son*, Henri Nouwen explored the painting by that same name by Rembrandt and the parable that inspired it. Chapters in his book view both painting and parable from the perspective of the younger, runaway son; the older, resentful son; and the forgiving and ever-vigilant father.

While it's tempting to think a parent could only relate to the father's love, there is much to be learned from the other two characters as well. The young mother who wanted "not to care so much" was tempted to leave it all behind through some form of escape. Parents are no less tempted than children to "run away from home." Some do, and the impact of their abandonment is shattering for those left behind, particularly the child. There is also the resentment that can grow around the demands of parenting, ones that don't often result in a mound of gratitude from the recipients of all that love and care. The guilt-inducing or pouting parent is a great vehicle for comedy figures like Marie Barone, the mother in the television show *Everybody Loves Raymond*. The reality of such a parent is no laughing matter, however.

The most intriguing chapter in Nouwen's book centers on the father. Rembrandt's painting depicts him bending over his repentant son in a gesture of compassion and caring. Two hands rest on the son's shoulders and constitute the heart of the painting. As Nouwen points out, the hands are quite different. One is strong and muscular—a father's hand that appears not only to touch but, "with its strength, also to hold." The other hand is smaller and more refined. "It wants to caress, to stroke, and to offer consolation and comfort." It is the hand of a mother.

This is not to say that a father doesn't console or that a mother doesn't stand strong. Instead, Nouwen is pointing out that the heart of love in the parable is both maternal and paternal. In his final chapter, he describes how we must each become like the father in order to love in openhearted fashion. In this beautiful parable, Jesus is not only describing the compassionate love of God for all of us; he also invites us to "become like God and to show the same compassion to others as he is showing to me." Accepting this invitation is no small matter. It takes the willingness to let go of one's own heart.

My own experience of parenting has been an education in love, one that often came in heartrending jolts as well as gentle nudges. I lost Jenny in one way; my other two children had their own moments of lost and found. Each one, in time, taught me how to become a more compassionate and merciful parent.

Tending the Heavy Heart

Jenny wasn't the only child I lost through death. When I suffered a miscarriage at the age of forty, I experienced a form of heartbreak for which I was totally unprepared. While I had mementoes from Jenny's short life—photos, clothing, and toys—there was nothing tangible with which to remember my fourth child, the one I never met. On top of that, a miscarriage didn't generate the same community support we received after Jenny's death. No communal prayers were offered for our baby, no visits received from the clergy or parish staff. It was a lonely and difficult time.

Anne Morrow Lindbergh, wife of the famous aviator, wrote an honest and heartbreaking memoir about the period of grief she experienced during and after the kidnapping and death of her baby, Charlie. She too found that one experience of suffering does not prepare us for another. "I used to think that having sorrow would make one feel more secure—as though you could say, 'Now I have borne suffering, I am strong, I will not be afraid again. Now the blow has fallen—I need not fear it again.' But it does not effect [sic] me that way, I feel all foundations shaking under me. I feel next to Death..." (*Hour of Gold, Hour of Lead*).

Every Christmas, we recount once again the account of Jesus' birth. We set up crèche sets depicting a gentle pastoral scene based primarily on the infancy narrative from Luke's gospel. These are populated with angels and shepherds and evoke the bright hope of new parents. Matthew's account is much darker. It details the slaughter of infant boys by a paranoid ruler and includes a gut-wrenching passage from the prophet Jeremiah to encapsulate the horror of that event. "A voice was heard in Ramah, wailing and loud lamentation, Rachel weeping for her children; she refused to be consoled because they are no more" (Matthew 2:18).

One of the most striking things about the prayers of lament in the Bible is how they often conclude with a prayer of praise or acknowledgment of God's presence throughout the experience. Hard as they are, times of suffering break us open to new realities and the presence of a God who not only stands strong with us but also weeps alongside of us. A heart open to love must also be open to loss. Once having experienced a devastating loss, no matter in what form, we may be tempted to close off to the potential for any more sorrow. This leads to a cold and shuttered heart. The paradox, however, lies in the openhearted response. Yes, we become more vulnerable, but we also find ourselves more resilient and compassionate. We also become aware of the miracle of resurrection—the great mystery of Christian faith. Life does arise out of death, light out of the darkest places. For Anne Morrow Lindbergh, it came with the arrival of a new baby. "I felt I had given birth to more than a baby: to new life in myself...And I felt as if a great burden had fallen off me."

As Parker Palmer describes it, one way to navigate the tragic gap is by going straight to the heart of our pain. This begs the question—how? How do we do this in a way that doesn't lead down the rabbit hole of deep depression? The movement across the gap is from the head—where we easily resort to rationalizing or to repetitive and self-recriminating thoughts—to the heart. It is here where we allow the pain to simply be rather than trying to think our way through it.

I find journaling to be a great help in this regard. When laden with grief, entangled in knots of anxiety, beset by guilt, or simply submerged in perplexity over a child's behavior, writing out my thoughts and feelings is a form of self-care. Reading over letters from past periods of struggle provides perspective and reminds me to take a longer view. Doing so helps me recognize God's presence in retrospect. Journaling takes many forms and can be as lengthy as a multipage letter or as simple as logging a thought or two. For introverts, in particular, this practice facilitates a way of giving voice to the cry within.

Palmer himself draws close to words in another way. Poetry, he writes, is one way to make his heart suppler and less likely to break into shards. Whether it's a psalm of lament or a verse by Emily Dickinson or Mary Oliver, the power of the poet to express the inexpressible is both consoling and heart-opening. Poetry is just one example of the outlet the fine arts provide during heavyhearted times. Henri Nouwen found a heart-opening experience through spending time with a parable and a Rembrandt painting. My husband, Ron, finds consolation in the lyrics of his favorite songs. In each case, the arts take us out of our heads and into our hearts, breaking them open to the light of grace and eventual healing.

The heavy heart also needs companionship, perhaps more than any other state of the heart. Confiding in a trusted friend or family member is a starting point. The listening ear of a spiritual director offers an opportunity to speak about one's pain in a safe and confidential manner. Sometimes the heart is far too heavy to carry without professional help. The counsel of a therapist can help parents deal with extraordinary burdens and problems that exceed their best efforts.

When Jenny was in the hospital, I came to a whole new understanding of intercessory prayer. Exhausted and anxious, I was uncertain about what or how to pray. I found myself letting go of particular formulas and took solace in Paul's description of the Spirit praying for us in "sighs too deep for words" (Romans 8:26). Others held me in prayer, keeping vigil with me in spirit. I am positive that those and other prayers throughout the years strengthened me for the long haul of parenting. This makes for another form of companionship during heavyhearted times. Praying for and with others, and allowing others to do so for us, not only provides strength to bear the burdens but opens the heart to hope.

QUESTIONS *for* REFLECTION *and* DISCUSSION

How have you experienced the heaviness of heart as a parent or witnessed it in someone else?

What other kinds of companions, gifts, and prayer help a parent whose heart is heavy with grief, anxiety, fear, or distress?

How has the experience of a heavy heart opened you up to mercy and compassion?

FOUR

The HOPEFUL HEART

RON AND I OFTEN JOKE THAT, INSTEAD OF GETTING UP ON SAT-
URDAYS TO ATTEND OUR KIDS' SPORTING EVENTS, IT WAS THE
OTHER WAY AROUND. Many was the morning when we roused
Eric and Anna before dawn and bundled them into the car
to head to one of Ron's trail races. I loaded up snacks, books,
and other items to keep them entertained during the long
wait for their dad to cross the finish line. Now that both of
them are on their own, I attend these races by myself. Lately,
I have become aware of the growing number of fathers who
are doing what I did all those years ago. They carry babies in
backpacks and navigate strollers through crowds bunched
around food tents and bandstands. Since Ron was a stay-at-
home dad during a time when it was still a rarity, the sight of

these fathers always warms the heart. This early interaction with children gives rise to hope in the bond of love that lasts for a lifetime.

Hope and Transformation

I once heard hope described as the "middle child" of virtues, caught between her two flashier sisters of faith and love. While definitions of faith and love are rarely misconstrued, hope is a bit more nebulous. It can easily be mistaken for optimism or wishful thinking. Often it sounds like a last resort. If a doctor tells you, "There is nothing to do now but hope," you know your days are numbered.

As a virtue, hope trusts in the present moment while it also looks to what can be. My favorite definition of hope is embodied in the beautiful words of Julian of Norwich: "All will be well and all will be well and all manner of things will be well." Received in one of her mystical visions, or "showings," the saying embodies a long-haul view of life. It isn't that all will be well today or tomorrow or even in one's lifetime. Instead, all will be well in God's time. Our ultimate hope as Christians lies in the incarnation as a continuing reality—the hope of Christ's constant coming. Only one who has experienced hope's transformative power can truly understand this.

Mary is one of those people. A great deal of time passed between her first encounter with the Holy Spirit and the last. She is named in Acts 1:14 as among those praying with the rest of the disciples in the upper room on the day before Pentecost. Artistic renderings of that event often situate Mary in the center of the disciples rather than to the side as would be expected of women in those days. Her wisdom and grace must have been a balm to those mourning Jesus' death, and a steadying force when the Spirit began enflaming hearts and blowing up a storm. After all, she'd had such a visit before! Mary is a model of what a disciple's heart must be—open, vulnerable, and steadfast. She displays the kind of courage and fortitude one must have to surrender the heart to the power of the Spirit.

One of the most curious things about Mary is that she is not among those mentioned as having a post-resurrection visit from Jesus. Perhaps she did and it was never recorded. It may be more likely, however, that she already knew of his new life in her heart. No need for placing her fingers in his hands, feet, or side. The great suffering she endured in the course of her life reached a transformational apex at Pentecost. The experience did not remove the sword from her heart but moved it deeper, splitting it wide open to the mysterious love of God.

Most parental experiences will come nowhere close to that of Mary's, but all have the potential for some kind of transformation. For the latter to happen, however, we have to become comfortable with ambiguity. I learned this when I set aside the *Better Homes and Garden Baby Book* in order to simply watch Jenny grow. From my current vantage point, I can see how the book was of limited help with Eric and Anna as well. None of my children progressed in step-by-step fashion. Just when I thought I figured out what ground we were on, the sand shifted under my feet. Holding things loosely became the best option. The best way to navigate one's way through parenting might be accepting the great mystery enfolded in the life of each child. It can be alternately delightful, devastating, or puzzling, but it's rarely boring. Thus, the great hope of parenting is the capacity to grow into it versus knowing from the get-go how it will all turn out.

Mystery into Mystery

In his song "Closer to the Light," Canadian songwriter Bruce Cockburn describes the experience of being knocked sideways by the power of a sudden death and the unknowable reasons behind it. The lyrics describe the intertwining of life and death as "gone from mystery into mystery...from daylight into dark. Another step deeper into darkness, closer to the light."

While I was still in the grieving process, a new life was quickening inside of me—Eric. That pregnancy was far different than Jenny's, however. Mixed with the joy of expecting another child was the risky aspect of love. I knew in brutal fashion how opening my heart to new life also meant the possibility of that life being taken away. Ron and I were still in the same apartment in Alaska, and the crib where Jenny died would hold our new baby. I was a bundle of mixed emotions.

One of the fiercest was fear. I didn't necessarily worry about having another child with Down syndrome. Quite the contrary. I felt in some ways as if we had been cheated out of the experience of raising a child with special needs and the discoveries we would have made about her and about ourselves. Far more difficult were memories of the hospital, the anxious days by her bedside, and the endless trips to and from the doctor's office in the final weeks of her life. If Eric was born with the same malady that eventually led to Jenny's death—something that was uncertain in the opinions of the doctors and surgeon—I wasn't sure I could endure it.

One day, while well into my second trimester, I went out for a walk. All of these anxieties trailed me as I made my way toward town. While passing a graveyard, I had a distinct impression of someone telling me my baby would be strong. It stopped me in my tracks. That "voice," wherever it came from, brought the same assurance given to Julian—simply that "all will be well." After that day, my anxieties lessened and I simply rested in the mystery of the unknown.

It was a striking occurrence at the time, to be sure, but became more so in the years that followed. Eric was born without any physical or mental disabilities and grew strong in will as well as in body. This posed its own set of challenges, to be sure. He grew mellower as a teenager, however, and developed an incisive wit along the way. A few years ago, he and I had the chance to visit Ireland together and being with him gave me a deep appreciation for his quiet strength and tremendous integrity.

Writer Jean Blomquist notes that we often only recognize the mysterious working of God in retrospect and from a vantage point of grace. From there we are able to acknowledge the presence of the Divine in ways we could not have done while caught up in the moment. "God quietly gathers in love the loose ends, tangled threads, and frayed edges of our lives and weaves them into a whole and holy fabric, richer in color and texture, more resilient in spirit and fiber than we can imagine" ("The Weaving and Wedding of Our Lives," *Weavings*, Volume VIII, No. 3). This is the graceful viewpoint of the parent of adult children—the *grand*parent. Whether he or she has actual grandchildren doesn't impede the greater ability to recognize, embrace, and celebrate the threads of God's love woven into a lifetime of parenting.

Companions in Hope

One of the greatest sources of consolation after Jenny's death was the love and support of our parish community in Alaska. After we returned from Denver, where Jenny was buried, the community held a memorial Mass for her. The familiar rhythm of ritual brought consolation during a devastating time. When Eric was born a year later, the same community celebrated his life with us at the time of his baptism. Both sacramental experiences embodied the hope that arises from being part of a community of faith.

The scene at Pentecost draws out the value of coming together as a community of believers in times of both sorrow and joy. The image of Mary and the disciples gathered in the upper room illustrates a very human way of coping with tragic and uncertain times. While we gather informally in homes during times of loss, the place of worship offers a centralized site for communal grief. As such, it provides a sanctuary in which to pray as one. Time-honored traditions as well as the strength of the faith community offer a beacon of hope in our darkest moments. The widespread use of the term "spiritual and not religious" falsely sets one against another. In truth, the rituals religious institutions do so well facilitate healing and offer hope during the worst of times. These include formal rituals, such as funeral rites and prayer services, as well as the informal ones, such as parish suppers and prayer circles.

The support of a faith community is not just a place to turn during times of trauma. It is also a day-to-day source of strength and encouragement for parents who strive to instill values and nurture faith in their children. I not only experienced this as a parent but also as a pastoral minister. Whether it was bringing families together for catechetical programs, preparing children to celebrate the sacraments, or participating in the Sunday Eucharist, I saw time and again the vital role of the parish in supporting, encouraging, and providing resources for parents.

In like manner, spiritual practices passed down through religious traditions are another source of hope for parents. These might be followed in a traditional manner or adapted to meet the demands of a busy family. Thus, it's not unusual to hear of the car being as much a setting for family prayer as the dining room table. Parents have told me about praying the Rosary using a phone app or listening to inspirational podcasts while waiting for kids at a sports event or dental office. Such practices become a lifesaver in the midst of a parent's busy life. They also hone the gift that nurtures a hopeful heart.

Wisdom and Hope

"All things happen for a reason." This catchphrase can be dismissed as a platitude or embraced as a deep piece of wisdom—it depends in large degree on the state of one's heart. If we want easy explanations for complex issues, we can simply surrender all hope as we sluff off difficult questions. Seen through the eyes of faith, however, we recognize the "reason" behind dark nights and difficult days as something more than fate. Hope gives us the capacity to see God's hand at work in our lives. The gift of wisdom guides us in this direction.

Wisdom is another of those daunting virtues, one that may conjure up images of gurus on mountaintops. It might better be described as a deep sense of knowing. Parents are often gifted with this wisdom in simple yet profound ways. They just know when something is awry or when to hold their tongue rather than speak. In a conversation with a stepfather, for example, I was taken with the description of his patience in the face of a stepson's adolescent anger. "Did he throw back at you the fact that you were not his birth father?" I asked. "Yes," he responded, "but I understood the issues were not about me. I just knew I had to stay present to him."

David Steindl-Rast uses the term "common sense spirituality" to describe the kind of awareness exhibited by the stepfather. It goes beyond thinking and comes straight from a wide-open heart. "It is a vibrating aliveness to the world, in the world, for the world. It is a knowing through belonging. And it becomes a basis for doing, for acting" (*Common Sense Spirituality*). Jim, a father of nine, described this inner knowing beautifully when he wrote about the joy of parenting from his perspective. "All is right with the world when I'm holding a sleeping child. The noise and problems fade in those quieted moments, and I feel so close to God."

This kind of awareness gives rise to another form of prayer particularly well-suited to parenting—that of blessing. Bestowing a blessing is an act of great tenderness. It affirms the love we have been given and the love we have for others and for God. When we acknowledge the blessings in our lives, we are not simply attributing them to a bit of good luck.

Instead, we embrace the gift of being held in God's heart, cherished for who we are rather than for what we do, say, or possess. Blessings recognize the divine spark of life in others and bring into greater focus the ever-present reality of God.

There is a transformative power in blessing not only the people but also the experiences in our lives. This makes them fitting prayers for the hopeful heart. In her book *An Altar in the World*, Barbara Brown Taylor writes, "To pronounce a blessing on something is to see it from the divine perspective." In such a manner, blessings arise from wisdom—the capacity for seeing things with a view toward God's will in our lives. In such a way, the one who blesses is often transformed in the process. This is what makes it such a hopeful form of prayer. Blessings offered throughout the various stages and states of parenting—from the terrible twos to the rebelliousness of adolescence, the wonder of birth to the pride of seeing a child graduate, wed, or become a parent—make it possible to see the hope abiding in all manner of things and how all is indeed "well." This is part of the surrender that is essential in openhearted parenting, a letting go into the great heart of God.

Tending the Hopeful Heart

In 2002, fourteen-year-old Elizabeth Smart was taken from her home in Utah and held captive for nine months. It was a horrifying experience for her and a frightening scenario for all parents. During that same period, a couple of other child kidnappings generated additional alarm. One day, I received a call from a woman in our parish undergoing a crisis of faith over these incidents. As the mother of a six-year-old, she was beside herself with anxiety and beset with questions about her faith. She asked how a just and loving God could allow such a terrible thing to happen to an innocent child. The best I could do was remind her of the power of hope.

The ancient symbol for hope is the anchor. Not only does it keep a boat from drifting out to sea but it can also be hauled up again, allowing the boat to sail. As such, it provides a balance between remaining entrenched by our fears and forever seeking an escape from them. Hope presages possibility. Steindl-Rast says that "only hope can build God's house… The house that hope builds combines in a unique way the security of love and the adventure of faith" (*Common Sense Spirituality*). Hope, he notes, is the daughter of twofold courage: the courage to build and the courage to build lightly.

This is easier said than done, particularly when caught up in worry and stress. How does one cultivate hope throughout the long-haul experience of parenting? What hope is there when life looks bleak for so many? What does it even mean to hope when I am just trying to keep my head above water? Paul offers a helpful response in his letter to the community at Philippi: let go and look ahead. "This one thing I do: forgetting what lies behind and straining forward to what lies ahead, I press on toward the goal for the prize of the heavenly call of God in Christ Jesus" (Philippians 3:13–14).

LETTING GO

It is important to remember our past, to be sure, but to do so in a way that grounds us in God's grace and love. The stories we tell ourselves about our own lives can keep us locked in place and frozen in fear. Letting go of guilt, of past mistakes, of resentments, anger, fear, or worry over what might happen is a liberating experience. To forget things behind doesn't mean we don't value our past but that we don't become enmeshed in it. Anne Lamott describes this as a "wow" experience because we keep getting to start over. "If we stay where we are, where we're stuck, where we're comfortable and safe, we die there. We become like mushrooms, living in the dark, with poop up to our chins. If you want to know what you already know, you're dying...You're saying: Leave me alone; I don't mind this little rathole. It's warm and dry. Really, it's fine. When nothing new can get in, that's death...New is life" (*Help, Thanks, Wow*).

When we are able to let go—to hold things loosely—we are able to see that life isn't set in stone, that blessings arise from the worst experiences, and that there is grace embedded in the wound. This is the kind of hope parents need when they fear their best efforts aren't enough, when the infighting at the dinner table becomes intolerable, when the tantrums and mood swings wear the nerves to a frazzle, or when raising a child seems like way more work than it's worth.

I once picked up a flower pot and found a crocus in full bloom beneath it. It exemplified the hope of a parent. Even when we feel like our efforts are futile or when we think we are failing miserably, we trust in something beyond our view. We hold on to hope that something is blossoming in the darkness. We let go of instant outcomes and trust in the process of growth.

LOOK AHEAD

As a runner, Ron has shown me the value of looking ahead

versus back. If he has a bad run or doesn't finish a race as expected, he doesn't dwell on it. Instead, he sets his sights on the next one. Like Paul, he presses on in faith toward the goal that lies ahead.

The Jesuit theologian and paleontologist Teilhard de Chardin wrote that evolution does not depend on a "push from below" but rather on a "pull from above." He identified this as the Omega Point. "God, in all that is most living and incarnate in him, is not far away from us, altogether apart from the world we see, touch, hear, smell and taste about us. Rather [God] awaits us every instant in our action, in the work of the moment" (*The Divine Milieu*).

What better way to describe parenting than "a work of the moment." The goal of parenting is not giving our children a happy childhood, wonderful as that is. It is moving them toward compassionate adulthood. How we do this varies according to our particular circumstances and the unique individuals in our care. The goal, however, remains the same, as does the need to entrust our children to God's care. Even in worst-case scenarios, we can pray them into God's heart with faith that all will be well in good time.

QUESTIONS *for* REFLECTION *and* DISCUSSION

How do you define hope? What kind
of hope does a parent need to have?

In what ways can or does a faith community
sustain a parent's hopeful heart?

How does letting go and looking ahead
give rise to hope in your life as a parent
or in the lives of parents you know?

PRAYER *for* ALL STATES *of the* HEART

Several years ago, I was asked to speak at a conference on contemplative prayer. When the speakers gathered together for lunch, I was seated next to a monk who asked me to describe my morning prayer regimen. I told him it revolved around the schedules of two young children. The best I could do was a quick bit of journaling or reading before they arose and the day began. He ruminated on this awhile and then said, "It seems like being a parent is a great impediment to the spiritual life."

When leading retreats for mothers, I find them incredibly interested in books, websites, phone apps, and other materials on prayer, reflection, and "everyday" spirituality. They want resources that speak to a parent's life and experience.

In her book *Sacred Dwelling*, Wendy Wright points out the challenge of finding these. Christian spirituality is a rich treasure trove for the heart and soul. Much of the writing, however, has been done by those living a celibate or monastic life. As a married woman and mother, Wright notes how much of this literature "either ignored my lived experience or disdained it as a context within which one could achieve spiritual maturity."

The importance of prayer in the spiritual life goes without saying. Even so, finding time to pray can be a challenge for a parent who is pulled in multiple directions. Far from being an impediment to the spiritual life, however, parenthood has its own spiritual rhythm. While I wasn't able to put into practice the traditional Liturgy of the Hours that punctuated the monk's day, I was able to find my own way in prayer that shifted as my children grew and our routines changed. I would even go so far as to suggest that a parent's way of praying might offer a benefit not found in a monastery. It *evolves*. When my children were infants and toddlers, they helped me appreciate the prayer of contemplation—a being in the moment in which I could simply rest in God. I recall the midnight feedings in which all was quiet except for the gentle sounds of my baby. Like the father holding his sleeping child, I too felt the closeness of God and how all was right in the world. As my children grew older and more self-sufficient, I moved into a different kind of prayer. Journaling took hold in a more regular fashion as a way to reflect on the blessings in my life. As the parent of adult children I take longer stretches of time for retreat and meditation. Parenting can be an entire education in prayer.

Single-heartedness

Of all the Beatitudes, my favorite is "Blessed are the pure in heart, for they will see God" (Matthew 5:8). Some translations use the word "single-hearted," which in Greek denotes wholeness, health, and simplicity. It also connotes generosity. Parenthood invites a single-heartedness that moves a person in radical ways toward giving one's heart to another. Transformation is the result. In her book *The Fountain and the Furnace*, Maggie Ross writes, "Our only task is to seek willingness... This radical willingness will, if we are faithful to it, shatter every idea we have about ourselves." As a parent of three children, I can personally attest to the way in which my own heart has grown in small yet steady increments over the years. Parenting draws us out of ourselves and gives us opportunities to grow deeper in faith, stronger in hope, and more richly in love than we can ever imagine. It gives us hearts of flesh.

RESOURCES

Godwin, Gail. *Heart: A Natural History of the Heart-Filled Life*. New York: HarperCollins, 2002

Hendricks, Kathy. *A Parent's Guide to Prayer*. Mystic, CT: Twenty-Third Publications, 2004

Hendricks, Kathy. *Prayers and Rituals for the Home*. New London, CT: Twenty-Third Publications, 2013

Lamott, Anne. *Help, Thanks, Wow*. New York: Riverhead Books, 2012

Lamott, Anne. *Grace (Eventually)*. New York: Riverhead Books, 2007

Lindbergh, Anne Morrow. *Hour of Gold, Hour of Lead*. New York: Mariner Books, 1993 Reissued

May, Gerald. *The Awakened Heart*. New York: HarperCollins, 1991

Muller, Wayne. *Learning to Pray*. New York: Bantam Dell, 2003

Nouwen, Henri. *The Return of the Prodigal Son*. New York: Doubleday, 1992

Palmer, Parker. *A Hidden Wholeness*. San Francisco: Jossey-Bass, 2004

Powers, William. *Hamlet's Blackberry*. New York: HarperCollins, 2010

Rolheiser. Ronald. *The Holy Longing*. New York: Doubleday, 1999

Ross, Maggie. *The Fountain and the Furnace: The Way of Tears and Fire*. Eugene, OR: Wipf and Stock, 2014 reprint edition

Steindl-Rast, David. *Common Sense Spirituality*. New York: Crossroad Publishing Company, 2008

Tannen, Deborah. *You're Wearing That?* New York: Random House, 2006

Taylor, Barbara Brown. *An Altar in the World*. New York: Harper One, 2009

Walter, Hal, *Full Tilt Boogie: A journey into autism, fatherhood , and an epic test of man and beast*. Out There Publishing, 2014

Weavings: A Journal of the Christian Spiritual Life. Nashville, TN: Upper Room Publications

Wright, Wendy. *Sacred Dwelling*. New London, CT: Twenty-Third Publications, 2015.

Additional Resources

"On Being"—Weekly radio program on National Public Radio, hosted by Krista Tippett. The focus of the program is spirituality. The accompanying blog, **www.onbeing. org/blog**, is a wealth of inspiration and insight.

www.gratefulness.org—Web site sponsored by the Network for Grateful Living includes reflections, prayers, practices, and a "word of the day."

www.webelieveandshare.com—Weekly blog by Kathy Hendricks and sponsored by William H. Sadlier, Inc. Each blog includes a downloadable prayer or reflection for use in the family or parish.